MOLLY E. ROSE

CONTENTS

INTRODUCTION

This business book is different.

Unlike every other book you'll read with titles like "How To Craft The Perfect Business Plan in 89 Incredibly Simple Steps", this book is different. It's a simple "How To" guide for creating a Business Plan that's right for you and your business and also an easy to follow workbook.

The workbook will guide you through the process you need to follow. It tells you the questions that you need to consider, the numbers you need (and how to get them), and supporting documents you need to gather.

The main purpose of a business plan is to aid YOU in running YOUR business. So the workbook has been designed for you to write the information in and refer back to as needed. If you need to supply your Business Plan to another party, such as a bank if you're looking for finance, then it's a simple to type up the various sections for a professional document.

Running your own business is both a challenging and daunting prospect. With a well-thought out business plan in place (anticipating the challenges you'll face AND the solutions) it will be much less daunting and much more exciting.

Good luck!

Molly

WHAT IS A BUSINESS PLAN?

In simple terms, a business plan is a written description of the vision for your business's future. That's really all there is to it. A document that describes (in as much detail as you or your investors need) what you're planning to do and how you plan to go about doing it. If you scribbled down a few lines of your business strategy on the back of a napkin, then you've written a plan (or at least the seed of a plan). With this workbook in your hands though you'll be able to do so much more.

So what do you need to include in a business plan? How do you actually put one together? Basically, a business plan states your goals, the strategies you'll employ to hit those goals, any potential challenges you foresee (and how you'll get over them), how you'll structure your business, and what investment you'll need and how you'll use it. Putting it together is the easy bit with this workbook!

WHY WRITE ONE?

Business plans are used for three reasons. (1) They objectively evaluate the feasibility of a new business idea. Is there a market for the product or service you'll be offering? How big is the market and can your team meet the goals you've set? Will the business make a profit and when will it start to break-even? (2) It also provides a blueprint showing how you'll run the business and how you'll overcome challenges. (3) It allows you to communicate your business idea to others for example your banker if you're looking for finance.

HOW TO WRITE YOUR PLAN

Writing a business plan is not something that you should try and knock off in a couple of hours. It's an important planning document for your business and you will get most value out of it if you allocate an appropriate amount of time to the process. It's not uncommon for many new businesses to spend 100 hours or more on the research and writing up of the plan. If this seems like a lot it's worth bearing in mind that planning will often uncover significant challenges that you hadn't previously considered. You'll then be able to work out the solutions on paper, rather than in the 'real world' when your business is operational. This is likely to save you many more hours (as well as monetary savings).

When you've completed this workbook your plan will have three sections:

1) The Words—this will describe how your business will grow and develop

2) The Numbers—this will show the financial data that backs up what you've said in the first section

3) Supporting information—such as resumes of the key people in the business, purchase orders for business you've already secured, drawings or maps of business premises you've located

KEY PLAN INFORMATION

This is a summary of the basic information about the business. Don't worry if you don't have some of it just yet (such as the business name or telephone number). You can always fill this in later.

Business Name: _____

_____

Address: _____

_____

_____

_____

_____

Website: _____

Contact email: _____

Phone Number: _____

Key Contact: _____

EXECUTIVE SUMMARY
(or IMAGINING THE BUSINESS)

In your final written-up business plan, the Executive Summary will be a page that gives an overview of the key information from your plan. It's used to give a quick summary to potential investors of what you're planning to achieve. Use this page to imagine what your business will look like when it's finally finished. What do you hope to achieve? Are there similar businesses you admire (and want to beat!) Let your imagination run wild. Don't worry, you don't have to show this page to anyone if you don't want to.

_____

_____

_____

_____

_____

_____

_____

_____

_____

_____

_____

_____

_____

_____

_____

DESCRIPTION OF THE BUSINESS

Always aim for clarity and simplicity when you're compiling your business plan. Use the 'Elevator Test' (explaining your business idea in the time to takes to go from the lobby to the 10th floor). Your job is to communicate your ideas simply so that people understand them quickly.

What general type of business is this?_____

_____

_____

What is the business legal form? Sole Proprietorship / Partnership / Corporation / LLC / Other

What are the products? _____

_____

_____

Who are the customers? _____

_____

What is unique about the business? _____

_____

Why will the business be successful? _____

_____

(Existing businesses) Why is the owner selling? _____

_____

PRODUCTS AND SERVICES

On this page describe the products and/or services that you'll be offering for sale. Include product features and an overview of any new technology or processes. If your product or service is unique, say why.

What products/services will you be selling? _____

_____

_____

_____

What are the key features and benefits? _____

_____

_____

What position do you want to occupy in the market? _____

_____

What makes your products/services unique and different from the competition? _____

_____

_____

Why will customers buy these products/services from your business?

_____

_____

MARKET ANALYSIS

For new and existing businesses, market analysis is essential to help justify the forecasted sales projections. Existing businesses can use past sales data, start-ups will need to rely on competitor observation, stats, and surveys.

Who buys your type of products or services? (Geographic, demographic, and psychographic characteristics) _____

_____

_____

_____

What is the size of the market and is it growing/shrinking? _____

_____

_____

What share of the market will you have? _____

_____

What is the industry outlook? _____

_____

_____

Are there customer groups who aren't served by the competition? _____

_____

_____

MARKETING PLAN

In this section you'll include the strategies you'll employ to develop and promote your products and/or services.

What are you selling? _____

_____

_____

What image are you trying to develop? _____

_____

What new products/services will you be introducing? _____

_____

_____

What will your pricing strategy be? How does this compare to your competition? _____

_____

Who are your target customers? _____

_____

What media will you use to tell them about your products/services? ___

_____

_____

What will this cost? _____

_____

LOCATION(S)

Business premises in prime areas will cost considerably more to rent or buy. On the flip side, prime locations may help attract customers (and therefore reduce your advertising costs). They may also give your business the premium image you're looking for. It may also be important to locate your business close to key suppliers, or to other complementary businesses.

What is (or will be) the business address? _____

_____

_____

If leasing, what are the terms? _____

_____

Are modifications/renovation needed? What will the costs be? _____

_____

_____

Describe the property and surrounding location: _____

_____

_____

_____

Why is this a good location? _____

_____

COMPETITION

One of the first questions an investor will ask is who your competition are, so it's important to have a clear answer ready. Be wary if you find that there are no competitors—is there a viable business? Remember to think as wide as possible here. Competition for a bowling alley will include leisure activities (such as restaurants and ice rinks), not just other bowling alleys.

Who are your key competitors? _____

_____

_____

_____

What strengths/weakness do you have vs these? _____

_____

_____

_____

How are these competing businesses performing? Are they struggling or expanding? _____

_____

_____

How will they respond to your new business? And how will you respond to that? _____

_____

MANAGEMENT & OPERATIONS

The success of many businesses (particularly new businesses) depends heavily on the performance of a small number of key people. So it's important to show that these are suitably qualified and experienced. Include resumes in the supporting appendices of a plan and if you're seeking finance then it can be useful to include personal financial statements.

What is the business experience of the management team? _____
_____
_____

Who is responsible for each functional area? _____
_____
_____

What is the reporting structure? _____
_____
_____

How will your products/services be produced? (Manufacturing processes, proprietary technology, key suppliers) _____
_____
_____
_____
_____

PERSONNEL

As your business grow how will you recruit, train, and retain good quality members of staff?

What are the staffing needs now and in the future? _____

_____

_____

_____

_____

What skills do they need? _____

_____

_____

_____

_____

What training will you provide? How will you deliver this? _____

_____

_____

_____

_____

What compensation packages will you give staff? _____

_____

_____

_____

APPLICATION AND EFFECT OF LOAN OR INVESTMENT

Whether you're applying for a loan, outside equity, or investing your own money, it's important to know what those funds will be used for and what effect they will have on your business. You will need to complete this section once you have filled in the financial data on the following pages.

What total investment is needed? _____

_____

How will the money be used? _____

_____

_____

_____

_____

_____

_____

_____

_____

When will the loan be repaid? _____

_____

What rate of return is possible for investors? _____

_____

FINANCIAL DATA

The main purpose of the financial projections over the following pages is to:

1) Determine whether the business is likely to be profitable

2) Calculate the level of capital investment the business will need and what it will be used for

3) Establish that the business is capable of generating cash to keep the operations going smoothly and to repay any loans

It is usually easier to complete the written sections at the beginning of this workbook first (the strategies and tactics you'll use to launch and grow your business). With these plans drawn up you can then more readily fill in the financial data.

With existing businesses filling in financial projections is much easier as they have past real data to draw on. For new businesses this is much harder. Use competitor knowledge, market research, and surveys to help you. Where there's no information available then use your best guess and write down the assumptions you make in your calculations. You can always revise the projections along the way but it is best to have A start point, rather than no start point at all.

INCOME STATEMENT

	1	2	3	4	5	6	7	8	9	10	11	12	Yr
Total Revenue													
Cost of Goods Sold													
Gross Profit													
Accounting & Legal													
Admin Salaries													
Vehicles													
Depreciation													
Equipment Rental													
Insurance													
Interest													
Marketing													
Office Supplies/Post													
Rent													
Repairs & Maintenance													
Payroll Taxes													
Utilities													
Total Expenses													
Pre-Tax Profit (Loss)													

Assumptions: _____

_____

_____

_____

BREAK EVEN ANALYSIS

Break Even or B/E Analysis is a very simple and yet incredibly valuable test of feasibility for a business or product/service. The purpose of the Break Even analysis is to determine what level of sales are needed to pay all the fixed costs and have zero income.

Use the following to calculate the Break Even for your business:

Variable costs are raw materials, packaging, and any other costs that change depending on the amount of production

Fixed costs are all other costs, i.e. those costs that are always there whatever the level of production such as rent, salaries, utilities

Unit Sales Price (P) =

Variable costs (VC) to product that unit =

Contribution Margin (CM) = (Price — Variable costs) =

Monthly Fixed costs (FC) =

Monthly B/E Sales (units) = FC / CM =

SOURCES AND USE OF FUNDS

This is a summary of how much money you need, where it will come from, and what it will be used for. This is a useful document if you are seeking outside investment in the form of loan or equity. Note that Total Sources must equal Total Uses.

Sources:	
Term Loan	
Line of Credit	
Personal Equity	
Outside Equity	
Other	
Total Sources	
Uses:	
Purchase Building	
Purchase Equipment	
Renovations	
Inventory	
Working Capital	
Cash Reserve	
Other	
Total Uses	

SUPPORTING DOCUMENTS

In your final Business Plan you will need to include a variety of supporting documents. The specific ones needed will depend on the nature of your business and the purpose of you Plan, for example you will likely need personal financial statements if you're seeking outside finance.

The following is a list of some of the documents you may need:

- Historical financial statements (for existing businesses)

- Tax returns (for existing businesses)

- Resumes of key staff members

- Reference letters

- Personal financial statements

- Letters of intent

- Purchase orders

- Contracts

CONCLUSION AND NEXT STEPS

Congratulations! Now that you've filled in all the pages of this workbook you'll have a robust plan and vision for your business. That might not seem like much, but it's a fact that most businesses don't have a business plan at all. They just hope to get along by "flying by the seat of their pants". Not exactly a recipe for success.

So now what? Well, that depends on what you need to do for your business right now. If the plan is for your own internal use then you can keep it in this draft form. Use the thinking you've put into these pages to determine the next steps you'll take for your business and then make a start.

If you're looking for outside investment, then type the document up and head over to see your bank manager.

Either way, make a commitment to re-visit your plan in 12-month's time to check your progress and adjust the plan (or your business) activities as necessary.

Good luck!

FURTHER NOTES

FURTHER NOTES

FURTHER NOTES

FURTHER NOTES

FURTHER NOTES

FURTHER NOTES

FURTHER NOTES

Made in the USA
Monee, IL
28 March 2022